How Heat Moves

Sharon Coan, M.S.Ed.

Consultants

Sally Creel, Ed.D.
Curriculum Consultant

Leann Iacuone, M.A.T., NBCT, ATC
Riverside Unified School District

Jill Tobin
California Teacher of the Year
Semi-Finalist
Burbank Unified School District

Image Credits: Cover & p.1 Fuse/Getty Images; p.11 Mike Tauber/agefotostock; pp.18–19 Kayte Deioma/Alamy; pp.6 (top), 12–13 iStock; pp.20–21 (illustrations) Janelle Bell-Martin; all other images from Shutterstock.

Library of Congress Cataloging-in-Publication Data

Coan, Sharon, author.
  How heat moves / Sharon Coan, M.S.Ed.; consultants, Sally Creel, Ed.D. curriculum consultant, Leann Iacuone, M.A.T., NBCT, ATC, Riverside Unified School District, Jill Tobin California Teacher of the Year Semi-Finalist, Burbank Unified School District.
    pages cm
  Summary: "When you run, you get hot. When you sit still, you get cold. Heat is always moving in and out of our bodies."— Provided by publisher.
  Audience: K to grade 3.
  Includes index.
  ISBN 978-1-4807-4568-1 (pbk.)
  ISBN 978-1-4807-5058-6 (ebook)
1. Heat—Juvenile literature. I. Title.
  QC256.C63 2015
  536—dc23
                                        2014013156

Teacher Created Materials
5301 Oceanus Drive
Huntington Beach, CA 92649-1030
http://www.tcmpub.com
ISBN 978-1-4807-4568-1
© 2015 Teacher Created Materials, Inc.
Made in China
Nordica.082015.CA21501181

Table of Contents

A Cold Day

It is cold outside. But you want to play. You wear a coat. You play hard and get too hot. So you take off your coat.

Then, you rest. But soon you feel cold again. You put on your coat!

Molecules and Heat Energy

Why does your body heat change? To find out, you need to know about **molecules** (MOL-uh-kyoolz).

You, Too!

Even you are made of molecules!

All things are made up of tiny bits called *molecules*. We cannot see them. But they are there and moving all the time.

Salt is made of molecules.

Water is made of molecules.

Heat is the **energy** of moving molecules. When they move quickly, they are hot.   When they move slowly, they are cold.

The molecules in this pot move quickly.

Moving molecules bump into each other. They share their energy when they do.

The molecules in these icicles move slowly.

What happens when hot and cold molecules bump? The hot molecules **transfer** some of their energy to cold ones. To transfer is to share.

The hot water makes food hotter.

Measuring Heat

We use a **thermometer** (ther-MOM-i-ter) to measure heat.

The hot molecules slow down. They get cooler. The cold molecules speed up. They get warmer.

Ice cream makes you feel cooler.

Your molecules move faster when you play hard. This warms you up.

These kids warm up as they run.

Your molecules transfer heat energy to the air around you when you rest. Your molecules slow down. You cool off.

This girl cools down as she rests.

Moving Heat

Some things transfer heat quickly. This means they **conduct** heat well.

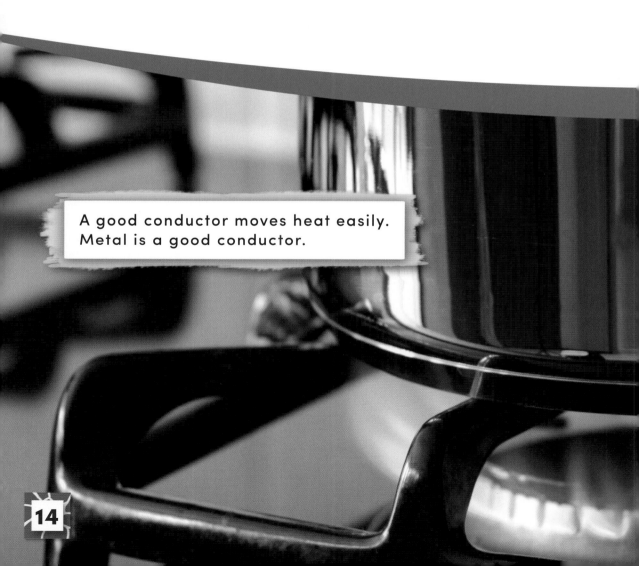

A good conductor moves heat easily. Metal is a good conductor.

Other things do not transfer heat well.
They are poor **conductors**.

Cloth is a poor conductor. It is hard for the molecules in your body to move the molecules in your cloth coat.

So the heat stays in your body. That is why we wear extra clothes when it is cold.

These kids stay warm because they are wearing coats.

Warming Up

You finish playing and go inside. Your mom gives you a mug of hot cocoa.

You put your hands around the mug. Can you feel the heat transfer to your chilly hands?

The heat from the cocoa transfers to her hands. They feel warmer.

Let's Do Science!

What can slow the melting of an ice cube? Try this and see!

What to Get

- ○ ice cubes

- ○ plastic bowl

- ○ things to wrap around ice cubes, such as foil, fabric, and a plastic bag

- ○ timer

What to Do

1. Wrap ice cubes in different things.

2. Place each wrapped ice cube into the bowl.

3. Wait half an hour. Then look at the ice cubes. What do you see? Which melted the least? Which melted the most?

4. Write what you think happened and why.

Glossary

conduct—to let heat pass through

conductors—things that will let heat pass through them

energy—the ability to do work or be active

molecules—tiny parts that make up all things

thermometer—a tool for measuring temperature

transfer—to move from one thing to another

Index

Your Turn!

Just Right

What kinds of hot food do you eat? What kinds of cold food do you eat? Do you eat more hot food or cold food? Keep a journal of the hot and cold foods you eat in a day.

How Heat Moves

When you run, you feel hot. When you sit still, you feel cold. Heat is always moving in and out of our bodies.

PHYSICAL SCIENCE

Lexile® 330L

ISBN 978-1-4807-4568-1
50000
9 781480 745681

TCM 21568